PART OF I

1705302719

'You can't con an honest man.'
So runs a classic swindler's maxim.
And 'You can't cheat death.'
And 'Not my will, but thine be done.'[1]

THERE IS NO INSCRIPTION on the gravestone of Benjamin Marks in Fairview, Iowa, other than his surname — though that in itself would stand as a perfectly apt and ironic comment on the man's achievements. The name is set off-centre below a carving of what appears to be a finely wrought corner of a temple building emerging out of (or descending into) a very rough hewn rock. It lends the façade an ambiguous spectral quality — the whole a poetic memorial to a delinquent window dresser.

---

1   The latter is the inscription on P.T. Barnum's grave, in Fairfield, Connecticut. The main memorial is an imposing 20-feet high structure topped with a portico and a giant urn and bearing the showman's surname in emphatic letters around a tiered plinth, set in a bed of brilliant flowers. Nearby, an incongruously modest footstone (actually the original grave) faintly bears this testimony of humility before God's will. It is tempting, though, to read that footstone/footnote as the showman's last prank on a gullible audience — giving them a spectacle offset by a deadpan acknowledgment that they sell themselves to the con, never the other way round. A con artist creates or emphasises the conditions in which a con is possible, but the final step into the trap is always propelled by the victim's will and vanity. It's an axiom that has held true through multiple paradigm shifts of travel and communication technology — each such shift promising to transform the notions of proximity and intimacy — each inadvertently creating as much potential for diversions as connectivity.

Ben Marks is acknowledged as the pioneer of the 'Big Store' — semi-permanent operations disguised as shops, banks, betting or Western Union offices for the purposes of elaborate cons. The stores thrived in the heyday of the American railroads and had a symbiotic relationship with the burgeoning infrastructure as it spread across America, particularly with the symbolic progress of the Union Pacific railroad as it forged through the Midwest heartland, pushing and trailing a caravan culture infamously labelled by newspaper editor Samuel Bowles as 'Hell on Wheels'.

The first historical record of Ben Marks has him as a 13-year-old messenger for the Union forces during the American Civil War — the course of this war was fundamentally altered by advances in transport and communication technologies, with early battles, such as that at First Manassas (Bull Run) decisively influenced by troops arriving by rail from distances hitherto way beyond the conceivable theatre of war. Abraham Lincoln started the war without a telegraph office at the White House and finished it by spending nights sleeping on the telegraph office floor. His telegraph style shifted too — starting with self-consciously formal 'letters' and growing sharper and more succinct as he learned the potential of the technology to instantaneously extend the sphere of direct command.

If Lincoln was something of an 'early adapter' — quick to grasp the potential of the new technology to change modern warfare, then Marks, the messenger boy indirectly in his employ, was a child of that technology, born four years after Morse's first 'What hath God wrought!' message. His inherited (and thus to him entirely natural) landscape was one of railway spikes moving inexorably westward, shortly to be matched by the staccato tempo markers of telegraph poles. It was a landscape of seemingly continuous expansion, yet one that featured rigidly fixed routes and interchanges that contained all the structural ingredients for particular social exchanges and economic extraction, on a sliding scale of legality. Council Bluffs, where he ultimately made his fortune, was situated just outside Omaha City and at one point was the fifth-busiest railway interchange in the country (and the Eastern starting point for the Union Pacific section of the transcontinental railroad). Under Marks' influence as a man about town (he was ostensibly a 'farmer and stockraiser', but in time came to be a powerful political fixer) Council Bluffs became known as a 'right town' by travelling con artists — a place where the local constabulary and judiciary had been paid off or intimidated and could be guaranteed not to make waves.

His most significant contribution to the con came earlier, however, in Cheyenne, Wyoming — the next important railway boomtown west of Council Bluffs. When Marks arrived there in the latter part of 1867, he was hustling a living by carrying a small folding table round his neck, that allowed him to set up a version of three card monte (aka 'Find the Lady') and to quickly flee the scene if challenged. As the railroad was painstakingly built through the Black Mountains towards Cheyenne, Marks was making small amounts of money from its advance cohort of speculators, railroad workers, prostitutes, gamblers, itinerant dancehall proprietors and fellow thieves — many arriving in anticipation of the next wave of more gullible victims from the moment the railroad reached the town, but in many cases finding themselves swiftly regulated out of town, or in one infamous case, in Laramie, Wyoming, driven out following a pitched battle with local vigilantes.

This itinerant advance guard adopted behaviours and expectations of success that were by nature transient. They might have brought 'Hell on Wheels' wherever they went, but those wheels kept turning — so that they were continually relocated at the exponential pace of the railroad's progress.[2] Marks was the first

2 As Wolfgang Schivelbusch has noted, they may not have been so distinct from the popular mythology of their fellow countrymen: The American 'is always in the mood to move on, always ready to start in the first steamer that comes along from the place where he had just now landed. He is devoured with a passion for movement, he cannot stay in one place; he must go and come, he must stretch his limbs and keep his muscles in play. When his feet are not in motion, his fingers must be in action; he must be whittling a piece of wood, cutting the back of his chair, or notching the edge of the table, or his jaws must be at work grinding tobacco... He always has to have something to do, he is always in a terrible hurry. He is *Grin* fit for all sorts of work except those which require a careful slowness. Those fill him with horror; it is his idea of hell'. (Michel Chevalier, *Society, Manners, and Politics in the United States*, 1839)

4

criminal to advance the mobile parasitic logic of the railroad grifter to match the ambitions of the host. He had noted the decision on July 4, 1867, by the chief Union Pacific engineer Grenville Dodge, that named the new town of Cheyenne as a future division point for the Union Pacific line. Dodge's vision of a monumental city at this junction inspired Marks to imagine more permanent structures to make money from the emigrants riding the iron horse west.

His initial invention was the Dollar Store — a shop front with a window full of gaudy merchandise apparently worth much more than the advertised dollar, but which existed purely as a lure for the greedy.[3] Inside the *Originally* shop an assortment of upturned barrels would be hosting various games of chance, usually monte, being followed by an enthusiastic crowd of 'gamblers', some of whom would seem to be enjoying conspicuous success. They were, of course, accomplices of Marks, and would lure the victims to try their luck and egg them on to higher and higher stakes. The rowdy and disorientating atmosphere would usually reach a physical crescendo in a surge out onto the streets of Cheyenne at the ultimate moment of loss, followed by a rapid dispersal that left the victims unaware they'd been conned, but suddenly aware they were alone.

The role of these accomplices would grow over time into that of skilled subcontractors for the principals directing the con. They would act as 'ropers',

---

3   Mention should be made here of L. Frank Baum, who, prior to writing one of the most popular allegories of the spectral operations of power in *The Wizard of Oz*, was a pioneer in the nascent art of window dressing — 1890s innovations in plate-glass manufacture having led to the possibilities of decorating windows like stage sets. In 1897 Baum established a magazine on the subject called *The Show Window - A Journal of Practical Window Trimming for the Merchant and the Professional*. Thirty years after Marks' initiative Baum observed of window dressing in general that 'the merchant who held out improbable and often impossible inducements drew the crowds, proving that the people... prefer a glaring uncertainty to a homely and modest surety'. Baum's 1901 story, *The Master Key*, about a boy who accidentally summons 'The Demon of Electricity' whilst experimenting with electric wires, was heavily plundered by spammers throughout 2004-2005 — copying text from out-of-copyright novels posted online, in order to pad their messages to get past software filters. One fragment that turned up in my inbox was the last line of the book: 'It's no fun being a century ahead of the times.'

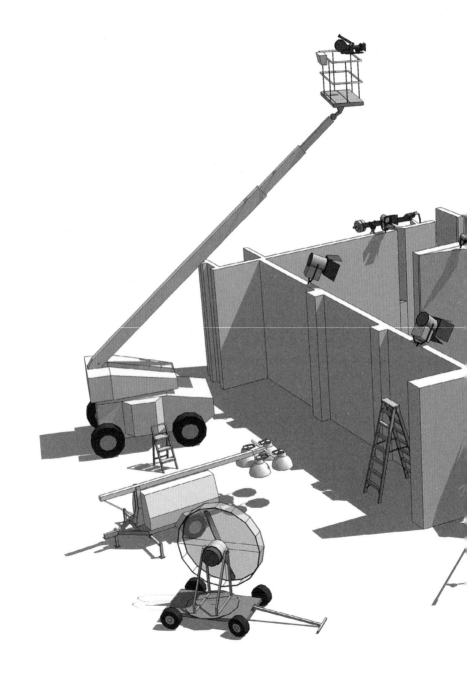

Cheyenne, Wyoming, 1867

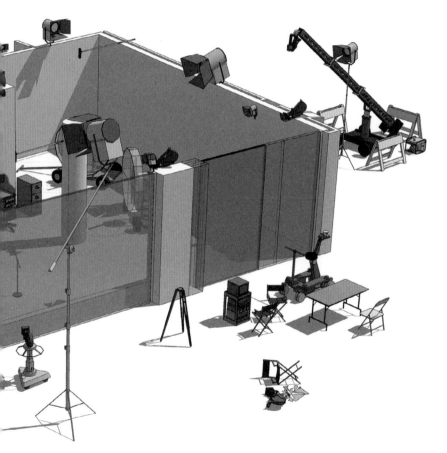

often acting alone and charged with befriending likely targets or 'marks', as they came to be known in honour of the Dollar Store's inventor. As the 'Hell on Wheels' era of westward expansion settled into a more mature phase of 'right towns' alongside a fixed transport infrastructure, the roping would move from the streets to the railway station and eventually to the trains themselves. As noted elsewhere, the American railway carriages were modelled more on the interior of steamboats than the stagecoach-inspired European models. This encouraged a degree of fraternisation on the American train that was not possible on its European counterpart. As one contemporary European observer put it, 'In this manner, a traveller is free to go and sit down next to whoever he likes, and also to change places again. An American would not much care for our way of travelling in a fixed seat, in a cramped carriage, under lock and key; he would sense a lack of air, of suffocation.'[4] Such an arrangement was ideal for the predatory roper:

The ease with which people make travelling acquaintances may account for the great number of marks which are roped on trains or ships. When a mark is off his home ground, he is no longer so sure of himself; he likes to impress important-looking strangers; he has the leisure to become expansive, and he likes to feel that he is recognised as a good fellow. The natural barriers to friendships with strangers comes down... And the roper knows how to play upon the festive note which is always latent in a traveller away from home. (David Maurer, *The Big Con*, 1940)

The forestalling potential of the railroad seemed infinite. Every day new people would be arriving in the new railroad towns, often with a large portion of their savings carried with them and *arriving at exactly the same point via a fixed route.*

---

4 G.T. Poussin, *Amerikanische Eisenbahnen* (1837), cited by Schivelbusch.

The earlier a roper intercepted them on that route, the more they could build the confidences required to steer their movements upon arrival. As the scams became more complex, and local law officials grew wiser to earlier versions, the further afield the ropers would travel in search of both anonymity and bigger scores — earning them the title of 'outsideman' and necessitating an ad hoc nation-wide cartel of stores to take advantage of their efforts.

These stores became more complex and mutated into the so-called Big Stores that had their heyday in the early part of the twentieth century. The logic behind the spectral frontage of the Dollar Store developed to govern all aspects of the stores, giving the mark a truly immersive fictional experience as they were robbed.[5] Capable of being reconfigured at a few hours' notice, the big store could be a Western Union office, a gentlemen's club, a numbers room, etc., depending on the needs of the con. Con men such as Ben Marks became impresarios, perhaps influenced by the theatrical model of the actor-manager, juggling repertoire and revenue alike. The metaphor would extend to the employment of 'extras' — travelling grifters who, upon arriving in a known right town without a con of their own in play, would ask around until directed to the local big store and the possibility of a walk on part in someone else's con.

The cons that were practised first physically disorientated the victim, then mentally unbalanced them, often by alluding to a complex series of temporal interventions on the telegraph system — fictional rigged delays allowing bets to be placed; engineered lags in delivering results, for unbelievable stock bargains to be had. As with all cons the mark was made a nominal accomplice in a scam — filling their head with useless logistics that prevented cool assessment of the situation and keeping them suspended in the belief that through 'intercepted' communications they were always a few minutes

---

5 David Maurer notes that at least one such store mutated into a legitimate Chicago department store when its owner discovered he could make more charging for inflated goods than from monte.

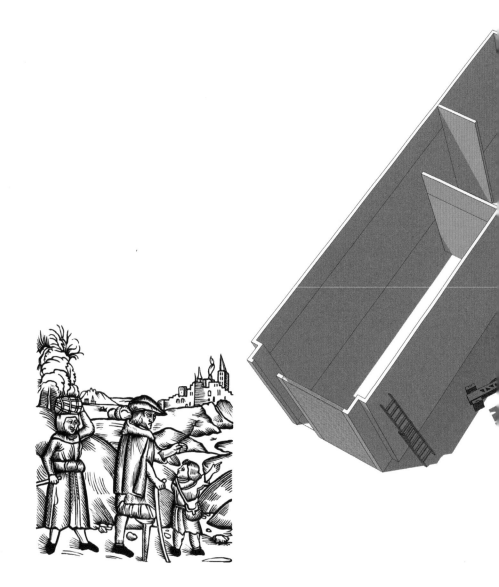

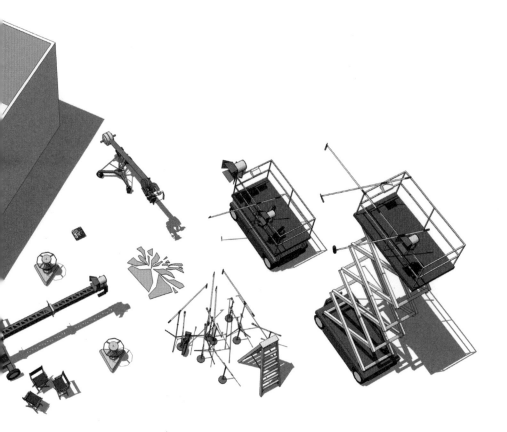

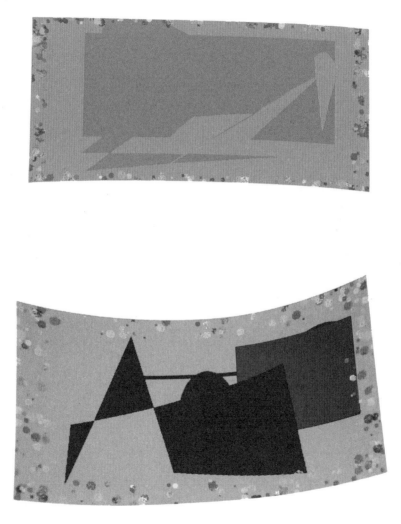

ahead of the average punter, when in fact they were suspended in
the parallel narrative arc of a well-made play.

This temporal dislocation was key in part since it played off an
emerging tenet of rail travel in relation to time — the idea that it regulated it.
Early rail journeys would involve arcane rituals, such as the routine for the
London-Holyhead mail train, where a pocket watch would be wound at the
Admiralty, placed aboard the train and then the mail boat to Dublin before
being wound and returned via the same route. Different stations within the same
country would run on different clocks, making uniform time-tabling impossible
— a situation that persisted in America until 1870.[6]

Gradually order prevailed and it was the logistics of railway expansion and
management that led it, offering the promise that their rhythms might in time
seem as natural as, say, the agrarian cycles that had once dominated much daily
experience. Writers from De Quincey onwards had offered accounts of rail
travel that spoke of the disturbing sense of a journey appearing to be over before
it began, effected by means that were mysterious to those who had once known
the visible exertions and pace of the horse. The most popular railroad cons
would promise their victims that they could exploit gaps in the totalising claims
of those who would regulate time and space on the communications networks of
America. The gaps were there of course and sometimes right where the con
artists said they were — but the true nature of the exploitation would be con-
cealed from the mark, even after they'd been fleeced.

There were three main cons: 'the wire', 'the pay-off' and 'the rag'.

The first of these, the wire, was invented just prior to 1900 and, true to the
gaming culture that spawned the Big Stores, it was a racing swindle. The wire
needed the use of two store spaces, one of which would be a fake Western
Union office, the other a 'horse-poolroom'. The con would shuttle the mark
between the two as it played out.

---

6 The adoption of 'Standard Time' was not confirmed until 1918. It was based on the five time
zones that had existed since 1870 for the management of the railroads.

The pay-off developed around 1906 and was a more baroque variation of the wire involving fake betting syndicates that claimed to have bought off the other runners in a horse race. This scam required a more complex organisation than its predecessor — even fictional claims require a corollary amount of administrative effort in a con. And the stakes and scenarios tended to be higher level, thousands rather than hundreds of dollars and private gentlemen's clubs rather than horse pool-rooms. These 'Long Cons' could last for weeks as the mark's resources were systematically drained. When this logic was extrapolated even further into the highest known form of American gambling, the stock market, the rag was developed.

The rag developed shortly after the invention of the pay-off, when con men found that the principle of this game could be applied to stocks and convinced the victim that the insideman of the mob was the confidential agent of a powerful Wall Street syndicate, which was breaking the small branch exchanges and bucket shops by manipulating the stock prices on the New York exchange... For the rag the store depicts a broker's office complete with tickers, phone service, brokers, clerks and customers. The same board which did duty for the races is often turned over to reveal a set-up for recording stock prices. (David Maurer, *The Big Con*, 1940) *Nonchalance*

The contemporary knowledge we have of these cons is due in large part to the efforts of linguist David Maurer — primarily known for his perennial bestseller *The Big Con* (which was the basis for the film *The Sting*). Maurer set out to write a linguistic study of the American criminal classes and in doing so inadvertently ended up writing *the* great field guide to the con trick in railroad-era America, framed by the argot its practitioners used.

Less well known but equally as interesting is his *Language of the Underworld* — a glossary of terms used by criminal and marginal subcultures — moonshiners, prostitutes, pickpockets and of course con artists. If the pleasure in reading *The Big Con* lies partly in the fact that Maurer clearly relished the milieu he described, without the disingenuously censorious tone that features in other underworld commentaries, *Language of the Underworld* sits rather more conventionally in an ongoing tradition of slang dictionaries.[7]

Many of these dictionaries and glossaries grew out of accounts of the inter-city migrations of the medieval period, prompted by war, disease and, in the case of the Jews, pogroms and Europe-wide edicts of expulsion and forfeiture of land. The perceived threat of roaming Jewish gangs at the city gates, guilty of everything from horse theft to poisoning the wells (a popular account of the causes of Black Death), was apparently compounded by the sound of the alien phrases these travellers used and continually adapted amongst themselves. The 1453 trial of the wandering Coquillard gang in France revealed references to such language but it was the first anthologies of Rotwelsch that really began to document these forms.

The predominantly Germanic language Rotwelsch drew on Yiddish, Romany languages, Italian and Judeo-Latin and was the main language of itin-erant classes from the middle ages onwards. First documented in the mid-thir-teenth century, by the late-fifteenth century it was known as the language or cant of false beggars and thieves. Rotwelsch was most famously documented in a slim volume called *Liber Vagatorum* (*The Book of Vagabonds and Beggars*), which was first printed around 1510, but which gained particular significance through the 1528 reprint, with its added authority of a foreword by Martin Luther (in which he emphasised the Hebrew influence on this language). Under Luther's influ-ence, the book was presented with an emphasis on addressing the problem of beggars via magisterial intervention − a role hitherto only ever imagined as the province of the church. But it also stands as an illuminating insight into the lyri-cal qualities of this language. Like all underworld slang Rotwelsch concerns itself primarily with descriptions about concrete transactions and goods, with little emphasis on abstract concepts. Yet, as with its twentieth-century American

---

7 This assertion on tone is perhaps reminiscent of Ibsen's dismissive claim in relation to the moral purpose of realism: '(Emile) Zola descends into the sewer to bathe in it. I want to cleanse it.'

counterpart, it was rife with poetic flourishes – to be arrested was to 'vanish into air', to get drunk was to 'buy the ape'.

Throughout the sixteenth to eighteenth centuries there were several published compendiums of English underworld language. 'Thieves' cant' was made familiar through the Elizabethan theatre and popular pamphlets of the time and its influence, as well as that of smatterings of Rotwelsch phrases, was still discernible by the time Maurer was documenting criminal argot in the railroad age. Cant was characterised as language used by a particular group, often for the purpose of concealing its meaning and usually with criminal intent. Contemporary slang largely derives from such language, though in a much rougher form and less determinate application. The very origins of the word 'slang' do still give a clue to the instrumental use of criminal languages though. It is believed to have been derived from a Norse verb *slengja* meaning 'to sling', particularly as in 'to sling one's jaw'. It developed as a description for loosely running one's mouth, perhaps using words to 'get in someone's face'. An intrusion and a distraction, *Impertinent* perhaps to disguise an agenda. It's a simple enough leap from there to envisage the street con artist's patter or even the functional text with which the spammer bypasses filters to deliver a marketing message.[8]

The principal cultural engines (at least prior to the emergence of the western teenager as a distinct social and economic group in the twentieth century) for these linguistic codes to develop and thrive, have traditionally been war and migration – moments of intensification, dispersal and new and precarious alliances. Ben Marks was born in just such a moment – coming of age carrying messages along the front lines of war, then making his fortune in intercepting the most advanced lines of communication of his day and diverting their users.[9]

---

8 'This is where the English language itself can be used as a spam evasion technique, where you can obfuscate words within different spellings, meanings, and suggestions. The example used earlier in this chapter was "Guess what I am pointing at you, thanks to my wondrous tablets." This used no known spam content, but was suggestive as to the focal point of the message – English-speaking readers would have few problems understanding what the message was referring to'. (Spammer X, *Inside the Spam Cartel*, 2005)

It wasn't inevitable that his name should become synonymous with his victims and become a term dispersed throughout the railroad network of America and eventually the world, but the conditions were certainly favourable.[10]

After leaving Cheyenne, Marks returned to Council Bluffs and spent the rest of his life doing all he could to ensure that this major railroad terminus was a model 'right town' — as productive a site for the con as any part of New York or Chicago. The big stores he inspired became a discreet feature of the streets surrounding many major railway terminuses across America — reaching their peak a decade after his death, during the Great Depression, when an abundant stock of abandoned offices and warehouses became available. Lag spaces to be stocked with confidence fictions, at a moment when general confidence was at its lowest.

The spectre of Marks is with us today. Hell online. Phishing scams (in which an e-mail purporting to be from a bank or financial institution invites you to link to a website to confirm your bank details) and to an extent Nigerian 419 scams can both be placed within the tradition of the Big Store. Marks and his contemporaries haunt our networks and language too — the travelling salesmen selling

---

9 Just three years after Marks' arrival in Cheyenne, the noted English playwright W. S. Gilbert (best known as the librettist of Gilbert and Sullivan) premiered the farce *Engaged*, in which a poor Scottish border family make a living by running a guesthouse for the distressed passengers of trains the family have derailed. Gilbert believed that the farce was the most perfectly mechanical of all artforms and that the actor in a farce showed the human being stripped back to their most atavistic animal state, just short of baring their teeth. Unbeknown to him, another mechanical form, that exploited this state, was being perfected in the American heartland.

10 Those conditions held potential for other directions too, of course. In the exact years corresponding to Marks' criminal apprenticeship as a denizen of Hell on Wheels, a young telegraph operator named Thomas Edison was holding down a series of temporary jobs throughout Midwest railway towns. Edison was already beginning to devise inventions that would first inadvertently underpin the con (the printable telegraph) and later undermine it. His electric motor, for example, would play a key role in the development of the car and the return of a more hermetic mode of travel in the European stagecoach tradition, rather than the American, post-steamboat, open rail carriage beloved by ropers. His phonogram and Kinetoscope too, would ultimately transform the regulated, mechanical experience of time and space ushered in by the railroads and create cinematic and archival spatial experiences unimaginable even for someone with Ben Marks' ability to intuit the inherent, if not advertised, qualities of a communication system.

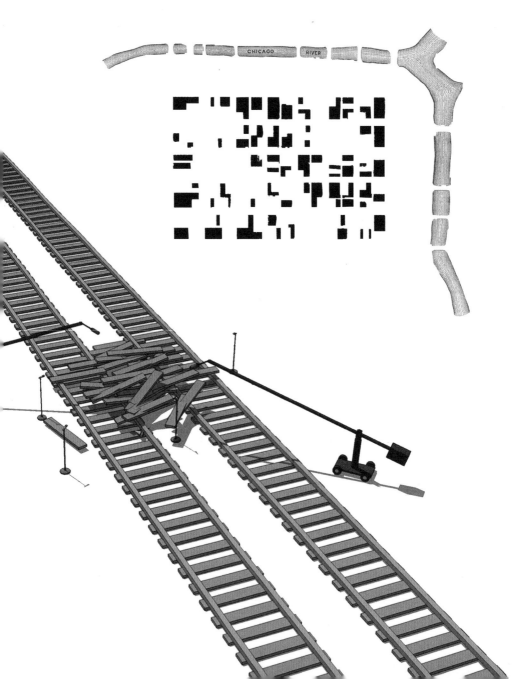

snake oil are selling it still, though these days the term refers to unnecessarily convoluted encryption software that offers no proven additional security.

Perhaps the single defining quality that 'marks' Marks as a contemporary figure is the amoral logic with which he assessed the potential of the network. When a Digital Equipment Inc. salesman named Gary Thuerk decided to promote a sales demonstration on May 1, 1978, by sending an electronic message to everyone on the Arpanet network, he miscalculated the formatting but was unrepentant about sending what came to be known as the first commercial spam e-mail, despite nearly crashing the nascent network as users scrambled to complain about what was then a huge message consisting mostly of other people's addresses.[11] Likewise, when the husband-and-wife lawyer team Canter & Spiegel advertised their Audacity Green Card services on over 6000 Usenet bulletin boards (regardless of relevance) on April 12, 1994, they brazened out the inevitable backlash (including the first coining of the word 'spam' in this context) and went on to write a book (*How to Make a Fortune on the Internet Superhighway*, 1995), positioning themselves as online marketing experts. It flopped, but they, or perhaps rather their Perl programmer 'Jason', had launched the era of mass commercial spamming.

And of course, when one thinks of 'the rag' con and its exploitation of the systems of stock exchange (or more accurately the systems that carried the news of those transactions as so much electrical chatter), it's impossible not to think of the contemporary shell games of derivatives and hedge funds, based on wonky computer algorithms that any farmer fresh off the train could see through (no market product underpinning the 'positions' . . .)

So yes, the mark is still with us.

Ben Marks is buried on a bluff.

The bluff faces out of the city, greeting travellers.

---

11 This message, the so-called DEC spam, is usually credited as the first spam mail, though at the height of the Vietnam War in 1971 a member of MIT's CTSS computing team sent a long message to the thousand or so members of the network, beginning with the anti-war activist A. J. Muste's statement, 'There is no way to peace. Peace is the way'. The unsolicited message is believed to have ushered in the first network safeguards — precursors of today's filters. cf http://spamassassin.apache.org/tests.html.

ILLUSTRATIONS

FRONT AND BACK COVER *Long Con*, Graham Parker, 2006. From a series of neon signs based on titles of spam e-mails.

INSIDE FRONT AND BACK COVER Sketch of American railroad network (sketch based on 1890 Census data); sketch for first node of Arpa network, September 1969.

PAGES 4, 5, 9, 14, 15, 18, 23 *Captchas 1-9*, Graham Parker, 2008. From a series of prints based on Edgar Allan Poe's nine qualities of the successful swindler (described in the 1850 essay 'Diddling Considered as One of the Exact Sciences'), as found in online 'captchas' (text-based tests to verify that a human is filling in a form, rather than a bot); cf. *419 (OCCASIONAL 420)*, p. 14, fn. 8.

PAGE 2 Benjamin Marks' grave, Fairview, Iowa.

PAGES 6-7 *Temple Bar sting*, Graham Parker, animation still, 2007 (from series based on occupying existing gallery spaces as sound stages set for classic cons).

PAGES 10-11 Frontispiece from *Liber Vagatorum*, 1528; *Burgin Sting*, Graham Parker, animation still, 2007 (from series based on occupying existing gallery spaces as sound stages set for classic cons).

PAGES 12-13 *Poststall 1 and 2*, Graham Parker, Giclée diptychs, 2008. Series of photographs shot from artist's studio window onto former Gair engineering works tramlines (in Vinegar Hill, Brooklyn) that are now popular backdrops for photo and film shoots. The artist 'parasites' onto these shoots and pairs the resulting photographs with images based on graphics from spam e-mails. Graphic e-mails were a briefly popular filter-defeating tactic in 2005-2006. Mostly used to promote 'penny stock' schemes, they would feature advertising text directly embedded into garish, crude graphics. The prints were produced by editing the text out and continuously photographing, re-colouring and re-printing the resultant image – a process the artist calls *adding pixel weight*.

PAGE 17 *Barnum* (detail), Graham Parker, 35mm slides, 2000. Two bricks from Little Ireland in Manchester carried to Lower Manhattan to recreate a publicity stunt in which an unnamed idler carried two bricks around the intersection outside Barnum's American Museum in a mute, enigmatic performance that drew attention to the museum entrance. The stunt took place in 1842 – the year Friedrich Engels published *The Condition of the Working Class in England* (based partly on walks through Little Ireland); cf. *Petrol Liar*, pp. 3 and 9.

PAGES 20-21 Background: *Pell Street Server* (detail), Graham Parker, Giclée print, 2005; foreground: *The Great Train Robbery* (stills), Thomas Edison, 1903; *Travelog 2* (stills), Graham Parker, digital video, 8 mins, 2006.

PAGE 22 *Engaged IV*, Graham Parker, lightbox image, 2006; *The loop*, Graham Parker, Giclée print, 2008 (drawing based on buildings with unknown owners, Chicago 1898).